Austin Dobson, Bernard Partridge

Proverbs in porcelain

To which is added

Austin Dobson, Bernard Partridge

Proverbs in porcelain
To which is added

ISBN/EAN: 9783337303747

Printed in Europe, USA, Canada, Australia, Japan

Cover: Foto ©Andreas Hilbeck / pixelio.de

More available books at **www.hansebooks.com**

Proverbs in Porcelain

TO WHICH IS ADDED

"AU REVOIR"

A DRAMATIC VIGNETTE

BY

AUSTIN DOBSON

" Rien en relief "

LONDON
KEGAN PAUL, TRENCH, TRÜBNER, & CO. L⁽ᵀᴰ⁾
PATERNOSTER HOUSE, CHARING CROSS ROAD
1893

TO

MY FRIEND

CHARLES B. FOOTE

OF NEW YORK.

PREFATORY NOTE

The six "*Proverbs in Porcelain*," here reprinted from "Old-World Idylls," *were first published in 1877 in a collection of miscellaneous verse. To these is now added, as belonging, if not to the same series, at least to the same species, the dramatic vignette called "Au Revoir,"* from "At the Sign of the Lyre." *I confess that I felt some misgiving whether these miniature studies, so frail in structure, so slight in substance, would lend themselves readily to pictorial embodiment. But this was clearly to reckon without the vitalising power of Art, and the accomplished pencil of* Mr. BERNARD PARTRIDGE.

AUSTIN DOBSON.

September, 1893.

CONTENTS

	PAGE
PROVERBS IN PORCELAIN	19
The Ballad à-la-Mode	23
The Metamorphosis .	35
The Song out of Season	47
The Cap that Fits .	59
The Secrets of the Heart .	71
"Good Night, Babette!" .	81
Epilogue	93
"AU REVOIR" .	97
NOTES	113

LIST OF ILLUSTRATIONS

"NINETTE! I feel *so* sad" .	*Frontispiece*	
"Grow eloquent on glaze and classing" (Prologue)	*To face page*	16
The Ballad à-la-Mode (half-title)	,,	20
"But there's some sequel, is there not?"	,,	24
"And no one dreams—of PERFIDY" .		28
The Metamorphosis (half-title) .	,,	32
"He fancies he's a LA FONTAINE!" .		36
"L'ÉTOILE,—by all the Muses!"	,,	40
The Song out of Season (half-title)		44
("No sound. I'll tap once more")		48
"IT WAS THE ABBÉ TI—RI—LI!"	,,	52
The Cap that Fits (half-title)		56
"Not young, I think" .		60
"And called (I think)—'The Cap that Fits'"		64
The Secrets of the Heart (half-title) .		68
"She used to tell us,—moonlight nights"		72
"Good Night, Babette!" (half-title)		78

LIST OF ILLUSTRATIONS

"BABETTE! I say! BABETTE!—BABETTE!!"	*To face page*	82
"Sing me your Norman *chansonnette*"	,,	86
"But we,—we are not always gay!" (Epilogue)	,,	90
"Au Revoir" (half-title)	,,	94
("How do they take it?—Can you see?")	,,	100
"BEAU-*vau?*—BEAU-*vallon?*—BEAU-*manoir?*"	,,	106
NOTES (half-title)	,,	110

PROLOGUE

'Grows eloquent on glaze and classing.'

PROVERBS IN PORCELAIN

PROLOGUE.

ASSUME *that we are friends. Assume*
A common taste for old costume,
   Old pictures,—books. Then dream us sitting,—
Us two,—in some soft-lighted room.

Outside, the wind:—the "ways are mire."
We, with our faces toward the fire,
   Finished the feast not full but fitting,
Watch the light-leaping flames aspire.

Silent at first, in time we glow;
Discuss "eclectics," high and low;
   Inspect engravings, 'twixt us passing
The fancies of DETROY, MOREAU;

" Reveils" and " Couchers," " Balls" and " Fêtes;"
Anon we glide to "crocks" and plates,
   Grow eloquent on glaze and classing,
And half-pathetic over " states."

Then I produce my Prize, in truth;—
Six groups in SÈVRES, *fresh as Youth,*
   And rare as Love. You pause, you wonder
(Pretend to doubt the marks, forsooth!),

And so we fall to why and how
The fragile figures smile and bow;
   Divine, at length, the fable under . . .
Thus grew the " Scenes" that follow now.

THE BALLAD À-LA-MODE

"*Tout vient à point à qui peut attendre.*"

SCENE.—*A Boudoir Louis-Quinze, painted with Cupids shooting at Butterflies.*

THE COUNTESS. THE BARON (*her cousin and suitor*).

THE COUNTESS (*looking up from her work*).
Baron, you doze.

THE BARON (*closing his book*).
I, Madame ? No.
I wait your order—Stay or Go.

THE COUNTESS.

Which means, I think, that Go or Stay
Affects you nothing, either way.

THE BARON.

Excuse me,—By your favour graced,
My inclinations are effaced.

THE COUNTESS.

Or much the same. How keen you grow!
You must be reading MARIVAUX.

THE BARON.

Nay,—'twas a song of SAINTE-AULAIRE.

THE COUNTESS.

Then read me one. We've time to spare:
If I can catch the clock-face there,
'Tis barely eight.

"But there's some sequel, is there not?"

THE BARON.

   What shall it be,—
A tale of woe, or perfidy?

THE COUNTESS.

Not woes, I beg. I doubt your woes:
But perfidy, of course, one knows.

THE BARON (*reads*).

"'*Ah, Phillis! cruel Phillis!*
(I heard a Shepherd say,)
You hold me with your Eyes, and yet
  You bid me—Go my Way!'

"'*Ah, Colin! foolish Colin!*
(The Maiden answered so,)
If that be All, the Ill is small,
  I close them—You may go!'

"*But when her Eyes she opened
(Although the Sun it shone),
She found the Shepherd had not stirred—
'Because the Light was gone!'*

"*Ah, Cupid! wanton Cupid!
'Twas ever thus your Way:
When Maids would bid you ply your Wings,
You find Excuse to stay!*"

THE COUNTESS.

Famous! He earned whate'er he got :—
But there's some sequel, is there not?

THE BARON (*turning the page*).

I think not—No.   Unless 'tis this :
My fate is far more hard than his ;—
In fact, *your* Eyes——

"And no one dreams—of Perfidy."

THE COUNTESS.

        Now, that's a breach!

Your bond is—not to make a speech.

And we must start—so call JUSTINE.

I know exactly what you mean!—

Give me your arm——

THE BARON.

        If, in return,

Countess, I could your hand but earn!

THE COUNTESS.

I thought as much.   This comes, you see,

Of Sentiment, and Arcady,

Where vows are hung on every tree . .

    THE BARON (*offering his arm, with a
        low bow*).

And no one dreams—of PERFIDY.

THE METAMORPHOSIS

" On s'enrichit quand on dort."

SCENE.—*A high stone Seat in an Alley of clipped Lime-trees.*

THE ABBÉ TIRILI.   MONSIEUR L'ÉTOILE.

THE ABBÉ (*writing*).

" *This Shepherdess Dorine adored*———"

What rhyme is next?   *Implored?—ignored?*

Poured?—soared?—afford?   That facile Dunce,

L'ÉTOILE, would cap the line at once.

'Twill come in time.   Meanwhile, suppose

We take a meditative doze.

(*Sleeps.   By and by his paper falls.*)

M. L'Étoile (*approaching from the back*).

Some one before me.   What! 'tis you,

Monsieur the Scholar?   Sleeping too!

(*Picks up the fluttering paper.*)

More "*Tales*," of course.   One can't refuse

To chase so fugitive a Muse!

Verses are public, too, that fly

"*Cum privilegio*"—*Zephyri!*

(*Reads.*)

"Clitander and Dorine."   Insane!

He fancies he's a La Fontaine!

"*In early Days, the Gods, we find,*

Paid frequent Visits to Mankind;—

At least, authentic Records say so

In Publius Ovidius Naso.

(Three names for one.   This passes all.

'Tis "furiously" classical!)

"*No doubt their Purpose oft would be*

Some 'Nodus dignus Vindice';

"Insane! he fancies he's a La Fontaine!"

'*On dit*,' *not less, these earthly Tours*
Were mostly Matters of Amours.
And woe to him whose luckless Flame
Impeded that Olympic Game;
Ere he could say an '*Ave*' *o'er,*
They changed him—like a Louis-d'or.
("*Aves*," and current coinage! O!—
O shade of Nicholas Boileau!)
"*Bird, Beast, or River he became:*
With Women it was much the same.
In Ovid Case to Case succeeds;
But Names the Reader never reads.
(That is, Monsieur the Abbé feels
His quantities are out at heels!)
"*Suffices that, for this our Tale,*
There dwelt in a Thessalian Vale,
Of Tales like this the constant Scene,
A Shepherdess, by name Dorine.
Trim Waist, ripe Lips, bright Eyes, had she:—

In short, the whole Artillery.

Her Beauty made some local Stir;—

Men marked it. So did Jupiter.

This Shepherdess Dorine adored . . ."

Implored, ignored, and *soared,* and *poured—*

(He's scrawled them here!) We'll sum in brief

His fable on his second leaf.

(*Writes.*)

There, they shall know who 'twas that wrote :—

" L'Étoile's *is but a mock-bird's note!*" [*Exit.*

The Abbé (*waking*).

Implored 's the word, I think. But where,—

Where is my paper? Ah! 'tis there!

Eh! what?

(*Reads.*)

The Metamorphosis.

(*Not in Ovid.*)

" *The Shepherdess Dorine adored*

The Shepherd-Boy Clitander;

"L'Etoile, by all the Muses!"

> *But Jove himself, Olympus' Lord,*
>
> *The Shepherdess Dorine adored.*
>
> *Our Abbé's Aid the Pair implored;—*
>
> *And changed to Goose and Gander,*
>
> *The Shepherdess Dorine adored*
>
> *The Shepherd-Boy Clitander!"*

L'ÉTOILE,—by all the Muses!

       Peste!

He's off, post-haste, to tell the rest.
No matter. Laugh, Sir Dunce, to-day;
Next time 'twill be *my* turn to play.

The Song out of Season

THE SONG OUT OF SEASON

"*Point de culte sans mystère.*"

SCENE.—*A Corridor in a Château, with Busts and Venice chandeliers.*

MONSIEUR L'ÉTOILE.   TWO VOICES.

M. L'ÉTOILE (*carrying a Rose*).

This is the place.   MUTINE said here.

"Through the Mancini room, and near

The fifth Venetian chandelier . . ."

The fifth?—She knew there were but four;—

Still, here's the *busto* of the Moor.

(*Humming.*)

Tra-la, tra-la! If BIJOU wake,

He'll bark, no doubt, and spoil my shake!

I'll tap, I think. One can't mistake;

This surely is the door.

(*Sings softly.*)

" *When Jove, the Skies' Director,*

First saw you sleep of yore,

He cried aloud for Nectar,

  ' *The Nectar quickly pour,—*

The Nectar, Hebe, pour! ' "

(No sound. I'll tap once more.)

(*Sings again.*)

" *Then came the Sire Apollo,*

He past you where you lay;

' *Come, Dian, rise and follow*

"No sound — I'll tap once more"

The dappled Hart to slay,—
The rapid Hart to slay.'"

(*A rustling within.*)

(Coquette! She heard before.)

(*Sings again.*)

" *And urchin Cupid after*

Beside the Pillow curled,

He whispered you with Laughter,

'*Awake and witch the World,—*

O Venus, witch the World!' "

(Now comes the last. 'Tis scarcely worse,
I think, than Monsieur l'Abbé's verse.)

" *So waken, waken, waken,*

O You, whom we adore!

Where Gods can be mistaken,

Mere Mortals must be more,—

Poor Mortals must be more!"

(That merits an *encore!*)

"*So waken, waken, waken!*

O YOU *whom we adore!"*

(*An energetic* VOICE.)

'Tis thou, ANTOINE?   Ah, Addle-pate!

Ah, Thief of Valet, always late!

Have I not told thee half-past eight

A thousand times!

(*Great agitation.*)

But wait,—but wait,—

M. L'ÉTOILE (*stupefied*).

Just Skies! What hideous roar!—

What lungs! The infamous Soubrette!

This is a turn I shan't forget :—

'It was the Abbé Ti-ri-li!'

To make me sing my *chansonnette*
 Before old JOURDAIN's door !
 (*Retiring slowly.*)
And yet, and yet,—it can't be she.
They prompted her.   Who can it be ?

(*A second* VOICE.)
IT WAS THE ABBÉ TI—RI—LI !
 (*In a mocking falsetto.*)
"*Where Gods can be mistaken,
 Mere Poets must be more,—
 BAD POETS must be more !*"

THE CAP THAT FITS

"Qui seme épines n'aille déchaux."

THE CAP THAT FITS

"*Qui sème épines n'aille déchaux.*"

SCENE.—*A Salon with blue and white Panels. Outside, Persons pass and re-pass upon a Terrace.*

HORTENSE.   ARMANDE.   MONSIEUR LOYAL.

HORTENSE (*behind her fan*).
Not young, I think.

ARMANDE (*raising her eye-glass*).
And faded, too:—
Quite faded! Monsieur, what say you?

M. LOYAL.

Nay, I defer to you. In truth,
To me she seems all grace and youth.

HORTENSE.

Graceful? You think it? What, with hands
That hang like this (*with a gesture*).

ARMANDE.

                      And how she stands!

M. LOYAL.

Nay, I am wrong again. I thought
Her air delightfully untaught!

HORTENSE.

But you amuse me——

M. LOYAL.

                    Still her dress,—
Her dress at least, you *must* confess——

'NOT YOUNG, I THINK'

ARMANDE.

Is odious simply! JACOTOT
Did not supply that lace, I know ;
And where, I ask, has mortal seen
A hat unfeathered!

HORTENSE.

    Edged with green!

M. LOYAL.

The words remind me. Let me say
A Fable that I heard to-day.
Have I permission?

BOTH (*with enthusiasm*).

    Monsieur, pray.

M. LOYAL.

Myrtilla (lest a Scandal rise,
The Lady's Name I thus disguise),
Dying of Ennui, once decided,—

Much on Resource herself she prided,—

To choose a Hat. Forthwith she flies

On that momentous Enterprise.

Whether to Petit or Legros,

I know not: only this I know;—

Head-dresses then, of any Fashion,

Bore Names of Quality or Passion.

Myrtilla tried them, almost all:

" Prudence," she felt, was somewhat small;

" Retirement" seemed the Eyes to hide;

" Content," at once, she cast aside.

" Simplicity,"—'twas out of place;

" Devotion," for an older face:

Briefly, Selection smaller grew,

" Vexatious! odious!"—none would do!

Then, on a sudden, she espied

One that she thought she had not tried;

Becoming, rather,—" edged with green,"—

Roses in yellow, Thorns between.

'If the cap fits—'

" *Quick! Bring me that!* " 'Tis brought. " *Complete,
Divine, Enchanting, Tasteful, Neat,*"
In all the Tones. " *And this you call——?* "
" ' ILL-NATURE,' *Madame. It fits all.*"

HORTENSE.

A thousand thanks! So naïvely turned!

ARMANDE.

So useful too,—to those concerned!

'Tis yours?

M. LOYAL.

Ah no,—some cynic wit's;

And called (I think)—

(*Placing his hat upon his breast.*)

" The Cap that Fits."

The Secrets of the Heart

"Le coeur mène où il va."

THE SECRETS OF THE HEART

" Le cœur mène où il va."

SCENE.—*A Chalet covered with Honeysuckle.*

NINETTE.   NINON.

NINETTE.

This way——

NINON.

No, this way——

NINETTE.

This way, then.

(*They enter the Chalet.*)

You are as changing, Child,—as Men.

NINON.

But are they? Is it true, I mean?
Who said it?

NINETTE.

SISTER SÉRAPHINE.

She was so pious and so good,
With such sad eyes beneath her hood,
And such poor little feet,—all bare!
Her name was EUGÉNIE LA FÈRE.
She used to tell us,—moonlight nights,—
When I was at the Carmelites.

NINON.

Ah, then it must be right. And yet,
Suppose for once—suppose, NINETTE——

NINETTE.

But what?——

"She used to tell us:—moonlight nights—
When 'twas at the Carmelites."

NINON.

Suppose it were not so?

Suppose there *were* true men, you know!

NINETTE.

And then?

NINON.

Why,—if that could occur,
What kind of man should you prefer?

NINETTE.

What looks, you mean?

NINON.

Looks, voice and all.

NINETTE.

Well, as to that, he must be tall,
Or say, not " tall,"—of middle size;
And next, he must have laughing eyes,

And a hook-nose,—with, underneath,
O! what a row of sparkling teeth!—

NINON (*touching her cheek suspiciously*).
Has he a scar on this side?

NINETTE.

Hush!

Some one is coming. No; a thrush:
I see it swinging there.

NINON.

Go on.

NINETTE.

Then he must fence (ah, look, 'tis gone!)
And dance like Monseigneur, and sing
" Love was a Shepherd ":—everything
That men do. Tell me yours, NINON.

NINON.

Shall I? Then mine has black, black hair,—

I mean he *should* have ; then an air
Half-sad, half-noble ; features thin ;
A little *royale* on the chin ;
And such a pale, high brow. And then,
He is a prince of gentlemen ; —
He, too, can ride and fence, and write
Sonnets and madrigals, yet fight
No worse for that——

                NINETTE.

                     I know your man.

                NINON.

And I know yours. But you'll not tell,—
Swear it !

                NINETTE.

            I swear upon this fan,—
My Grandmother's !

NINON.

And I, I swear

On this old turquoise *reliquaire*,—

My great,—*great* Grandmother's!—

(*After a pause.*)

NINETTE!

I feel *so* sad.

NINETTE.

I too.   But why.?

NINON.

Alas, I know not!

NINETTE (*with a sigh*).

Nor do I.

"GOOD NIGHT, BABETTE!"

" Si vieillesse pouvait !—"

SCENE.—*A small neat Room. In a high Voltaire Chair sits a white-haired old Gentleman.*

MONSIEUR VIEUXBOIS. BABETTE.

M. VIEUXBOIS (*turning querulously*).
Day of my life! Where *can* she get?
BABETTE! I say! BABETTE!—BABETTE!!

BABETTE (*entering hurriedly*).
Coming, M'sieu'! If M'sieu' speaks
So loud, he won't be well for weeks!

M. VIEUXBOIS.

Where have you been?

BABETTE.

Why M'sieu' knows:—
April!... Ville-d'Avray!... Ma'am'selle ROSE!

M. VIEUXBOIS.

Ah! I am old,—and I forget.

Was the place growing green, BABETTE?

BABETTE.

But of a greenness!—yes, M'sieu'!

And then the sky so blue!—so blue!

And when I dropped my *immortelle*,

How the birds sang!

(*Lifting her apron to her eyes.*)

This poor Ma'am'selle!

M. VIEUXBOIS.

You're a good girl, BABETTE, but she,—

"Babette! I say! Babette!—Babette!"

She was an Angel, verily.

Sometimes I think I see her yet

Stand smiling by the cabinet;

And once, I know, she peeped and laughed

Betwixt the curtains . . .

    Where's the draught?

   (*She gives him a cup.*)

Now I shall sleep, I think, BABETTE ;—

Sing me your Norman *chansonnette*.

   BABETTE (*sings*).

  "*Once at the Angelus*

   (*Ere I was dead*),

  Angels all glorious

   Came to my Bed;—

  Angels in blue and white

   Crowned on the Head."

  M. VIEUXBOIS (*drowsily*).

"She was an Angel," . . . "Once she laughed".

What, was I dreaming!

> Where's the draught?

BABETTE (*showing the empty cup*).

The draught, M'sieu'?

M. VIEUXBOIS.

> How I forget!

I am so old! But sing, BABETTE!

BABETTE (*sings*).

"*One was the Friend I left*

Stark in the Snow;

One was the Wife that died

Long,—long ago;

One was the Love I lost . . .

How could she know?"

M. VIEUXBOIS (*murmuring*).

Ah, PAUL! . . . old PAUL! . . . EULALIE too!
And ROSE! . . . And O! "the sky so blue!" . . .

'Sing me your Norman chansonnette'

BABETTE (*sings*).

"*One had my Mother's eyes,*

Wistful and mild;

One had my Father's face;

One was a Child:

All of them bent to me,—

Bent down and smiled!"

(He is asleep!)

M. VIEUXBOIS (*almost inaudibly*).

"How I forget!"

"I am so old" . . . "Good night, BABETTE!"

EPILOGUE

'But we are not always gay.'

EPILOGUE

Heigho! how chill the evenings get!
Good night, NINON *!—good night,* NINETTE *!*
  Your little Play is played and finished;—
Go back, then, to your Cabinet!

LOYAL, L'ÉTOILE *! no more to-day!*
Alas! they heed not what we say:
  They smile with ardour undiminished:
But we,—we are not always gay!

"Au Revoir."
A Dramatic Vignette.

"AU REVOIR"

A Dramatic Vignette.

Scene.—*The Fountain in the Garden of the Luxembourg.*
It is surrounded by Promenaders.

Monsieur Jolicœur.   A Lady (*unknown*).

M. Jolicœur.

'Tis she, no doubt.   Brunette,—and tall :
A charming figure, above all!
This promises.—Ahem !

The Lady.

Monsieur ?
Ah ! it is three.   Then Monsieur's name
Is Jolicœur ? . . .

M. Jolicœur.

Madame, the same.

The Lady.

And Monsieur's goodness has to say? . . .
Your note? . . .

M. Jolicœur.

Your note.

The Lady.

Forgive me.—Nay.

(*Reads.*)

"*If Madame* [I omit] *will be
Beside the Fountain-rail at Three,
Then Madame—possibly—may hear
News of her Spaniel.* Jolicœur."
Monsieur denies his note?

M. Jolicœur.

I do.

Now let me read the one from you.

"*If Monsieur Jolicœur will be
Beside the Fountain-rail at Three,
Then Monsieur—possibly—may meet
An old Acquaintance.* '*Indiscreet.*'"

The Lady (*scandalised*).

Ah, what a folly! 'Tis not true.
I never met Monsieur. And you?

M. Jolicœur (*with gallantry*).

Have lived in vain till now. But see:
We are observed.

The Lady (*looking round*).

I comprehend . . .

(*After a pause.*)

Monsieur, malicious brains combine

For your discomfiture, and mine.

Let us defeat that ill design.

If Monsieur but . . . (*hesitating*).

M. JOLICŒUR (*bowing*).

Rely on me.

THE LADY (*still hesitating*).

Monsieur, I know, will understand . . .

M. JOLICŒUR.

Madame, I wait but your command.

THE LADY.

You are too good.   Then condescend

At once to be a new-found Friend!

"How do they take it?—Can you see?"

M. Jolicœur (*entering upon the part forthwith*).

How? · I am charmed,—enchanted. Ah!
What ages since we met . . . at *Spa*?

The Lady (*a little disconcerted*).

At *Ems*, I think. Monsieur, maybe,
Will recollect the Orangery?

M. Jolicœur.

At *Ems*, of course. But Madame's face
Might make one well forget a place.

The Lady.

It seems so. Still, Monsieur recalls
The Kürhaus, and the concert-balls?

M. Jolicœur.

Assuredly. Though there again
'Tis Madame's image I retain.

THE LADY.

Monsieur is skilled in . . . repartee.

(How do they take it?—Can you see?)

M. JOLICŒUR.

Nay,—Madame furnishes the wit.

(They don't know what to make of it!)

THE LADY.

And Monsieur's friend who sometimes came? . . .

That clever . . . I forget the name.

M. JOLICŒUR.

The BARON? . . . It escapes me, too.

'Twas doubtless he that Madame knew?

THE LADY (*archly*).

Precisely. But, my carriage waits.

Monsieur will see me to the gates?

M. Jolicœur (*offering his arm*).

I shall be charmed. (Your stratagem
Bids fair, I think, to conquer them.)

(*Aside.*)

(Who is she? I must find that out.)
—And Madame's husband thrives, no doubt?

The Lady (*off her guard*).

Monsieur de Beau——? . . . He died at *Dôle!*

M. Jolicœur.

Truly. How sad!

(*Aside.*)

(Yet, on the whole,
How fortunate! Beau-*pré*?—Beau-*vau*?
Which can it be? Ah, there they go!)
—Madame, your enemies retreat
With all the honours of . . . defeat.

THE LADY.

Thanks to Monsieur. Monsieur has shown
A skill PRÉVILLE could not disown.

M. JOLICŒUR.

You flatter me. We need no skill
To act so nearly what we will.
Nay,—what may come to pass, if Fate
And Madame bid me cultivate . . .

THE LADY (*anticipating*).

Alas!—no farther than the gate.
Monsieur, besides, is too polite
To profit by a jest so slight.

M. JOLICŒUR.

Distinctly. Still, I did but glance
At possibilities . . . of Chance.

THE LADY.

Which must not serve Monsieur, I fear,
Beyond the little grating here.

M. JOLICŒUR (*aside*).

(She's perfect. One may push too far.
Piano, sano.)

(*They reach the gates.*)

Here we are.

Permit me, then . . .

(*Placing her in the carriage.*)

And Madame goes ? . . .
Your coachman ? . . . Can I ? . . .

THE LADY (*smiling*).

Thanks ! he knows.

Thanks ! Thanks !

M. JOLICŒUR (*insidiously*).

And shall we not renew
Our . . . "*Ems* acquaintanceship ?"

l.

THE LADY (*still smiling*).

                                                    Adieu!

My thanks instead!

M. JOLICŒUR (*with pathos*).

                                It is too hard!

(*Laying his hand on the grating.*)

To find one's Paradise is barred!!

THE LADY.

Nay.—"Virtue is her own reward!"

                                              [*Exit.*

M. JOLICŒUR (*solus*).

BEAU-*vau*?—BEAU-*vallon*?—BEAU-*manoir*?—

But that's a detail!

(*Waving his hand after the carriage.*)

                              AU REVOIR!

Notes

NOTES

NOTE 1, PAGE 24.

"*Nay,—'twas a song of Sainte-Aulaire.*"

It is but just to the octogenarian Marquis, whom the Duchess of Maine surnamed her '*vieux berger*,' to say that he is guiltless of the song here ascribed to him. For it, and the similar pieces in these *Proverbs*, the author is alone responsible. In the *Secrets of the Heart*, however, he has, without attempting to revive the persons, borrowed the names of the charming heroines of *A quoi rêvent les Jeunes Filles*.

NOTE 2, PAGE 105.

"*A skill Préville could not disown.*"

Préville was the French Foote, *circa* 1760. His gifts as a comedian were of the highest order, and he had an extraordinary faculty for identifying himself with the parts he played. Sterne, in a letter to Garrick, from Paris, in 1762, calls him 'Mercury himself.'

www.ingramcontent.com/pod-product-compliance
Lightning Source LLC
Chambersburg PA
CBHW020151170426
43199CB00010B/985